Drugs Today-

Getting High or Trying to Die

BY: Lavoy Allison

Dedication:

To: Selena for making me once again believing in hugs and not drugs and loving me no matter what I do. Also for beating on me to make me take better care of myself. With love Snuggle Bunny

To: My family for always taking me back when the side affects got so bad I would run away.

To: and to my readers for buying this book and taking a serious look into what you are really doing to your body. Trust me you will want to spread the word that all you are doing is trying to get cancer and mentally illness. I pray for you! If it is drugs you need please read my book Cannabis: Bonsai Techniques and Why also on Amazon.

Table of Contents

Chapter 1: Right to Get High

I am forty-two and I smoked my first joint when I was five. I had a concussion and it helped ease the pain until the swelling went away. I have tried other drugs to I am not afraid to admit it. When I enlisted for the Air Force I signed up for the Special Forces job. When I went back to swear in I was met by a recruiter of the C.I.A. I had been writing the government offices like the Governor of Tennessee and up to the White House. Anyway that is another book all together. At seventeen I was given the title Honorary Doctor and assigned to do what I could to legalize street drugs that could be used as medicines. I also made Special Forces but like I said that is another book all together.

I am weird if you ask my old high school friends. I like to smoke cannabis and do math problems and study. That is the kind of person you have to be to last in this world and to get a job with the C.I.A. I worked hard but because of some of the people that do drugs I got poisoned. Some people you just can't talk sense into or make sense of what they do.

Someone I thought I could have as a friend helped poison me and I never did figure out why he would smoke posioned weed and stay with his other friend. Later I found out his other friend was related to the local law enforcement that was more like a big cartel. It took me fifteen years to get that cartel busted and not all of them went down.

Something you need to know they don't tell you to Just Say No because the drugs are bad for you it is that bad people but bad chemicals in street drugs all over the world to make you addicted. When I tried to sale cannabis in high school I noticed I had every kid in school that did drugs coming to me because I would not resale bad drugs just pure medical cannabis.

The only reason I was selling to other classmates is because they were getting poisoned by other dealers and I was being their doctor that didn't ask so many questions. When the other drug dealers had people to try to get me busted or they wanted me to pay for their cannabis to medicate I got out of selling.

That is when I noticed something strange to me. Some people didn't care what they were putting in their bodies. They would smoke weed laced with embalming fluid and say it was a great high. To be straight up with you putting something in your body that peaks death and say it is a great high is just someone that is suicidal trying to take as many as they can with them. Needless to say with that influence in Tennessee I still haven't gotten even medical cannabis legalized there.

Think about it with the people that are trying to get you 'high' to get you sick on these poisoned drugs and then keep you as a buyer the government isn't going for it. It is like K2 you are smoking weeds sprayed with embalming fluid and it will and is killing you. Embalming fluid (just the smell) will cause brain and lung cancer. K2 will cause mental illness and breathing problems if you live through your first experience. I believe the nazis are just out to get veryone dead or supported by the government. But what do I know about it I am just a C.I.A. agent and honorary doctor right!?!

Chapter 2: K2 What is it You Do?

Ah, K2 the drug of the streets of today. I held two tokes or inhaled twice and I blacked out for 2 hours and couldn't move. After that I found out what it came from. Embalming fluid! The only chemical I know of that you can get elbalming fluid in on the streets I asked the government to ban. The problem with that is the politicians have been paid off and I don't think I have gotten word to President Donald Trump yet. I do believe if it is in his power he will end it. After all the medical bills the government is paying is up because of the chemical warfare in this country of the United States alone.

K2 can cause cancer of the brain and lungs. Have you ever met anyone that is dying of brain or lung cancer. I have and it is the most depressing thing. As suicidal as they were they all wish that they would have done it different and stayed away from the shit! Some people cuss the Lord because they haven't got their prayers answered and then they rebel. After they calm down and the Lord answers their prayers they have cancer and they realize they are going to lose everything and their lives for what they did. Life sucks enough so stick with the Good Lord even when he is slow and use medical cannabis you dumb asses! I mean that in the sweetest way. Like I was yelling it at my family truthfully.

Now lets get into the mental illness side of things. Why would you purposely go out and get schizophrenia and try to hear voices that are going to drive you insane? That is what is going to happen when you smoke that K2 or Spice or anything else that is man made. Stick to medical cannabis. Trust me I am the closest thing to a doctor that is not a doctor but yet have done the shit! I am telling you to help get that shit off the streets. If nothing else by not buying it and telling everyone what you read in this book.

I asked a guy for some cannabis one day. You know what he tried? He tried to convince me that smoking potpourri was a great high. Again I realized that the world of getting high has changed. I thought stupid people could never take over the world but they have. The politicians have let the people that sell poisons as drugs take over the drug dealing business and the closest they have come to fighting this war is allowing some states to legalize cannabis. It is these people that poison the drugs that caused dispensaries to get most of the rights to sale cannabis. It is so you get pure cannabis and are safe. Some people in the government do love you so pray for them.

 The thing the federal government has come to see that some people do not care about themselves enough to take care of their selves and respect others well being. Knowing that why would they want to legalize cannabis or any other drug for people to poison others on a bigger scale. That is why it is taking so long to get cannabis legal in all states and we haven't ventured into the other drugs like heroin, meth, and cocaine. If it was a perfect world people could go to dispensaries and get the drug or drugs they needed and go home and ease the pain what ever it may be.

 When is this going to happen? I might see it in my life time but there is going to have to be some dumb brats get wise and call it quits. Some of the drugs getting to the streets is there because cartels poison them to get the cops that bust them and then use the shit. I about got shot by a couple of cops I tried to get to confess and tell who they were getting their drugs from so we could help them. After that I smelt gun powder. That K2 can make you stupid. They are using these poisons to destroy the country and they are beginning the zombie apocalypses. Look at your friend about to hand you that K2 and wonder when he or she is going to turn. Scares the fuckin' shit out of me dude!

Now that you have read all this realize that there is no and I repeat no medical purpose for K2, Spice, or anything synthetic. You can believe that shit!

Chapter 3: Holy Meth Factory

Okay admit it when you tried your first score of real Ice or cystal meth you thought it was the holy grail of speed use! I did, no shit! It has efedrin in it and it helps open your lungs so you get more oxygen to your muscles and you can go and go and keep going. But have you had medical meth? I have and that stuff is smooth!

If you are using the shake and bake method, using Heat gas treatment or Draino you have no idea what real meth is or what it is made of and that is a fact. You are following a nazi's way to make it that was making it for the local cops. And he smoked it until he was stupid and handled his drugs to a state trooper instead of his wallet in a traffic stop. I have met the man that started the rumors about the meth in soap and draino being where to get things to get high or make meth.

Yes the word meth is on a bar of soap but if any of you had taken chemistry and paid attention then you would know the truth. Meth is a chemcial compound bond that contains a certain number of elements. Say tri clolide meant three(tri) elements then meth meth (is like over fifteen elements). What about Draino well yeah you have another chemical used to make crystal meth. It is Iodine. Also found in Iodized Salt or table salt if you will. Last but not least Heat gas treatment. Yes it has alcohol in it but so does vodka. The only reason Heat was ever used was because one of the first meth cooks was under age and couldn't buy vodka.

Why do you need alcohol or vodka? Because again if you ever studied chemistry then you know that alcohol is used to make a compound combine if and only if the elements make a solution. In this case it does. Wouldn't it be safer to just mix your efedrin salt and vodka, stir until you make it a solution and then use a stove to evaporate the vodka(alcohol evaporates faster than water and that is why it is used in chemical solutions) and leave a crystalize meth compound? I know because that is Medical meth.

What does it taste like you ask? Like a smooth hit of almost air. No chemical taste or flamable fumes to kill you. With all the lies on the streets and anti-government groups you can see why the government hasn't even said a word to the public about legalizing crystal meth. As sad as it sounds, how I see it would make a cool name for a band but it is happening in real life. Suicidal zombies are controlling the drug trade and no one has a positive study of meth but me I guess. I had to put it in a book to get people to listen.

If you will follow my lead here and understand the real medical benefits of first efedrin and how easy it is to give in doses as crystal meth. Efedrin is used to cure the flu, pneomonia, and malaria but doctors are not telling the truth because the pharmiceutical companies have them by the balls. It was President George Bush Jr. I wrote to get it illegal for pill companies to give doctors a percentage of the sales of the drugs they prescribe. I got poisoned for telling by a doctor too. Back to point you can see there are reasons that meth can be used to treat people and should be studied further.

Just remember I am only an honorary doctor not a certified doctor that can prescribe drugs. I wish I could go to Washington D.C. and kick the shit out of some of the surgeon generals that have worked there. I kept a heifer cow (a female cow that hasn't had calves) from dying when she was on her last day of life. She had pneomonia and fell against the side of the stall in the barn. The owner was going to get the gun and I asked for one chance. I gave her four Head's Up pills (75% efedrin) also know as White Crosses or Speed and gave three to the owner to give her the next day. The last time I was on that farm she had twin calves and the owner thanked me.

Chapter 4: Heroin, Chasing the Dragon

Okay so I have seen a pure heroin tar ball once in my life. I never really had pain bad enough to need something stronger than cannabis but in my studies I came across it once. I rolled the heroin tar ball around on a piece of alumium foil and 'chased the Dragon' as they say. I took about three hits and folded it up. The guy I had got it from was an addict because he overused the drug. I didn't and you are about to hear my thesis from that study.

The guy I got it from was a boss of mine that owned a tree service company. I was labor and did a lot of lifting plus I have have the Old Author joint pain. I ache all the time so I told him I would try it to help along with my studies to legalize some of the street drugs. I asked about the side affects and the bad talk about the drug and he told me that after using for days you get sick without it. When I tried to put it up after three hits he got mad and when I said I was saving the rest for later he fired me.

Luckily his wife was there to make him hire me back and she told me to go on home and be ready for work the next day. I didn't get sick and the pain went away. I didn't ache the next day either. So you know the doctors are even pushing drugs that have way to much opium in the pills like oxies and all. Did you know that oxicodone is about eight doses and it should be administered as so. But the doctors are making money and many don't care! Now it is killing people.

Do you know what happens when you flood the brain with too many chemicals? You crash and it takes days or even weeks to feel better. Like I said I smoked a little, three hits to be honest and I was good for a day and a half. As long as you don't get a dealer like I dealt with that wants you to smoke all you have all at once and get sick by going so far as to bully you into it you will be fine most of the time. Unless you get fintinol. Or should I say anthax for you all to really understand.

What are you talking about you ask? I am talking about some doses of anthax which is pee from the most deadly frog in the world.

This frog can touch you and before you can say help you are dead. It is from Africa and it has been an adapted warfare technique by the nazis that are being hunted by all the governments even Russia.

Think about it, the shot you get through the chess for anthax is the same technique used for fintinol overdose. As a war technique they put that frog's pee on a crushed asprin. Take a bag of oxicodone pill material and throw in that crushed asprin. A 400 to 1 mixture and you shake well and name it something else. You get the street drugs that have been killing people.

Why has the government not released this information. Because they get enough problems from both sides as it is. The way we have seen people run to poisons people label as drugs knowing it will kill them has brought me to a conclusion. I calculate that 54% or more of drug users are suicidal willing to take others with them and that scares me. That has been my report to the government. That is really most of what I have seen on the streets.

Even though I have submitted most of what is in this book to the government nothing has been said about legalization about any other drug publicly. So will you see leaglized heroin packets in the dispensaries anytime soon? I doubt it!

Chapter 5: Vaporizers, Don't Toke No Joke

When you think of reasons to use an electronic cigarette what comes to mind? That it is cheaper, cooler because it don't smell, or safer. All of these are things people say but are you really getting safer nicotine? I would say no. No because I have not heard the electronic cigarette juice producers say anything about getting that nicotine or juice from organically grown tobacco! Plus if you are a true blooded smoker then it is a waste of time and money.

I have had better luck with rolling my own cigarettes. I can get a one pound bag of Red River pipe tobacco and three boxes of menthol tubes and I am good to go. It takes about $80 to get started but that is $54 for a cigarette rolling machine and $17 for the one pound bag of pipe tobacco and $10 for Cigarette tubes. That is the rolling paper with a filter in it and you are good to go. With three boxes of cigarette tubes that is three cartons of cigarettes a month. A box of tubes rolled is a carton of cigarettes.

 So you are not getting a better deal. You are not getting a safer product than cigarettes because they are using the same tobacco that is getting sprayed with the tobacco insecticide that causes cancer, breathing problems and makes cigarette smoking sound so bad. Say again, why do you want to use a vaporizer? I would just look for an organic tobacco seller on the internet and roll my own. I have been around tobacco farms and smoking since I was ten.

 My grandfather told me the story of how his grandfather was a doctor and why they hand out cigars when a baby is born. It is because smoking kills germs and it keeps the baby from getting diseases from you and others that smoke. I sent word to the Surgeon General to study a germ in a smoked filled tube and see. No word from them!?! I will smoke Red River pipe tobacco and live happy because I am sure if they don't change they use safer tobacco.

 I have smelt tobacco that was over sprayed with insecticides and they stick and cause you a sore throat. Also you can smoke a Winston cigarette or a Prymiad and they smell like chemicals burning. That is the insecticides coming through. Red River does not carry their signature taste and smell. I couldn't smell any chemicals in them but that was in 2016 and it is 2019 as this book is being written.

 So basically I am trying to let you know the safer ways to get your fill. I am not going to tell you that you shouldn't smoke at all. With the government not enforcing the use of organic insecticide I am not suggesting you smoke either. Remember I was named an honorary doctor and I stressed hard in school from the 4th grade up. I wanted to smoke at school in class it was so stressful! I will not shit you or pull your chain. The government seen a war coming and started the move away from people doing drugs. It is terrorism in this country and other countries that these drugs and unsafe products are on the streets and shelves of our stores.

 At the same time I want you to know I see your point I am also going to tell you I don't want you to get your fill on just anything. If we are going to take back this country we have to get safer drug dealers and drugs on the streets. Even some of the tobacco stores have a selection that they 'say' is organic so give it a try.

Just help us as the government is having to deal with all the drug users most likely are going to be on medicare and not able to work for a living. Yes I know that may not be the case with vaporizers but it is meant to be part of the message behind this book. Again I am going to ask. Why did you think vaporizers were better? I don't get it! I love to smoke so I had to go back to actual cigarettes.

Love yourself enough to get something that is not going to kill you as fast at least. When I don't roll my own I smoke 305 Menthol Cigars at a $1.60 a pack. The brown paper they use is paper made from tobacco stalks not beached wood. They last longer and will get you that fill without as many chemicals. Smoking is the way I lower stress, blood pressure, curve my appeitte, and kill time. I understand that some of you will consider what I say and some won't but I tried.

Chapter 6: Whats Up With That?

So why is it that many of the youth of this country are suicidal and out to use poisons and kill themselves. I don't get it. I love all people and I love you too. Does that help? I was a foster child at one time and I have had more than one family in my life. I know what it is like to not feel loved by family or who I had to claim as family. But all in all I gave the Lord my heart, body, and soul. It worked for me but I still had that pain. I medicated with cannabis and liked it a lot.

Seeing that I liked it a lot it was easy for people that thought I was a cop to poison me with the cannabis I was smoking. Oh yeah, I got poisoned at nineteen and had to learn to read, write, and talk again. I survived but I went through hearing voices and seeing things and the only thing that helped was cannabis. Did I get a prescription for medical cannabis being an honorary doctor and all? No. I had to spend time on probation and be seen as a druggy that couldn't beat the habit.

I wish I could have made things better for me but I couldn't. I used my words in letters with research of what was wrong with me to do something though. I mailed my thesis and self explaination of what I was going through, the voices, seeing things, and the headaches to the Surgeon General. Two weeks later I was announced as an honorary doctor on the news and was helping the Surgeon General get medical cannabis legalized for California.

I was sick but I was proud of myself. When you love to sing, dance, make people laugh and laugh yourself losing all that kills you inside and you lose God in your heart. I did anyway. I was trying to get myself killed and hated just about everyone and everything. I guess it was because I gave my heart to Lord God at a young age and meant it wholehearted I didn't lose my sight and go to killing myself with poisons. I have the love in my heart again and am an advocate for other with mental illness and proud of it.

So why do you that use this crap on the streets try to kill yourselves that way. Hell if life is that bad get in the military and do life the right way. Full force living and sadly sometimes dying for others. God will not be mad with you if you serve and do it wholehearted. It will earn you the braggin' rights to mouth off at times too!

Basically what I am saying is stay with us in this life and do not destroy your life for nothing on poisons. Lord God will not have mercy on you so he said to me. I love him and therefore I love you too. At least enough to tell you this truth.

Chapter 7: Cannabis, Is it Right For Me?

So now you are about to the end of this book. If you are still wanting to 'get high' maybe you are thinking about using medical cannabis. As an honorary doctor I thank you. That is about the only drug that will make you healthier as you 'get high!' I pray most of you are waiting until you have legal age rights to use and not using before hand but I know in this day and time that is a lot to ask for. Hell even grade school and high school are hard work. But that is no reason to take the chance and go out to someone and buy death in a bag trying to get high and escape your problems.

If you are going to use be honest with your parents and build that safety net so that if things get worse like you getting poisoned drugs they know what is going on. Most of the time they are going to tell you no but that is because they love you. Those of you that have parents that are okay with it, well be safe. As I have said people do poison drugs even spray cannabis with tobacco insecticide and say it is because of bugs.

 I have grown outside once and no bugs touched my plant. I was even using sugar and Juicy Juice mixed in water for fertilizer. I got the seed from a bag of regular street weed. It was Loud weed after all the natural organic fertilizer! Three hits and I was high for hours.

 I helped raise my nieces and I noticed that it wasn't doing any good telling them not to do drugs or not to do a lot of things as far as that goes. That is why I am taking a different approach with this book and life because I know that most people are going to do it anyway. I am writing this book because I love my country and I hate seeing what is happening especially to the youth. Poisoned drugs is the cause of over an estimated 1.2 trillion a year in medical bills.

 It is hard to find youth that want to work and enjoy life in love. The Lord made this world for all of us to do our part and that includes supporting yourself and controlling yourself. When I say controlling yourself I am talking about not partying life away and learn to use only when you need it. Yeah the first few times I did enjoy the funny laughs but I didn't let my grades fall. I didn't miss work to get high and I didn't forget to tell mom and dad I love them. That is the important things to remember but there is more to it than just those few things. I do hope you get the point though.

So remember to talk to the Lord the next time you do drugs and ask him if it is safe. As long as you aren't neglecting to feed your kids or pay your rent he will most likely be okay with it. Why do I say that? I was sick one time where I was around one of those fake meth labs that cops have to wear the suits for. I asked the Lord what was going to make me better and I looked down and found a quarter bag of cannabis. That was all he had to say to me!

Lord God is a cool motherfucker if you are good to others and follow the laws which are based on the ten commandments. Drugs were meant as medicines but drugs have been used to poison people especially kids so you know now the reason behind the drugs laws during this war on our country.

Medicate responsibly and be safe. Thank you for reading my book and God bless you all!